Love, Dad

Love Letters from the Heavenly Father's Heart

Ken LaPoint

Copyright © 2014 Ken LaPoint

Love, Dad
Copyright © 2014 by Ken LaPoint

All rights reserved. No part of this book may be reproduced or transmitted in any form or by any means without written permission from the author.

ISBN-13 978-0692227749 (Father's Heart Books)

Library of Congress Control Number: 2015900125
CreateSpace Independent Publishing Platform,
North Charleston, SC

Unless otherwise indicated, all Scripture quotations are taken from the Holy Bible, New Living Translation, copyright © 1996, 2004, 2007, 2013 by Tyndale House Foundation. Used by permission of Tyndale House Publishers, Inc., Carol Stream, Illinois 60188. All rights reserved.

Scripture taken from the HOLY BIBLE, NEW INTERNATIONAL VERSION®. noted by "NIV". Copyright © 1973, 1978, 1984 by International Bible Society. Used by permission of Zondervan. All rights reserved worldwide.

Scripture quotations are from the ESV® Bible (The Holy Bible, English Standard Version®), copyright © 2001 by Crossway, a publishing ministry of Good News Publishers. Used by permission. All rights reserved.

GOD'S WORD is a copyrighted work of God's Word to the Nations. Quotations are used by permission. (GWT)

Dedication

To my wife Annie, thank you for always listening to what Holy Spirit pours out to me. Thank you for being encouragement, being affirmation and being love. I have the privilege to write this book, but we share in the journey.
I love you.
Ken

INTRODUCTION

"Going a little farther, he fell to the ground and prayed that if possible the hour might pass from him. "Abba, Father," he said, "everything is possible for you. Take this cup from me. Yet not what I will, but what you will." Mark 14:35-36

"So you have not received a spirit that makes you fearful slaves. Instead, you received God's Spirit when he adopted you as his own children. Now we call him, "Abba, Father." Romans 8:15 Many equate Abba with our title, "Daddy".

Two of the most influential people in the Bible- two that had personal encounters with our Heavenly Father. Jesus and the Apostle Paul both chose to use this name for God that spoke of personal relationship. They addressed the God of all creation as, "Daddy".

The night before his crucifixion, Jesus called out in his hour of greatest struggle to "Abba", his Daddy. Paul encourages us to call upon God with the very same endearing name.

Jesus calls us to have the faith of a child; Paul tells us to have such a relationship with God that we can't help but call him Daddy.

I've been called Father for a long time. But there's something very close, personal and very special about being called "Dad".

A dad didn't just bring you into this world. He walks with you in this world. A dad will reveal his heart. A dad is a father who walks in love and his children know it! When a child receives a note signed, "Love, Dad", there is something profoundly important being given. That child knows to whom he belongs.

Dear reader, our God longs to have a relationship with you. He longs to be so much more than Lord and Savior.

He placed his very Spirit within you so you can know him as Daddy.

This book is letters of love that God spoke to me during my times alone with him. May they ignite conversations between you and our heavenly Father. May they reignite the first love that drew you to Jesus when you first met him.

This book is not to be a replacement for your personal times with our Lord and Savior, but rather something that will encourage you to go closer and deeper in your relationship with him. I encourage you to find a regular, daily time with your Bible, a journal and a pen- expecting for Dad to show up and to share his heart with you- things worth remembering, things worth writing down.

The Father truly loves you,
Ken

P.S. Nothing written herein is intended to contradict God's Word, the Bible. May his letters to me be an encouragement for you to seek him every day and to hear his voice. His sheep do know his voice.

Love, Dad

Contents

Introduction — v
   Contents — ix

Love, Dad — 1
   I Never Fail to Love You — 1
   Your Last Two Cents — 2
   Faith that Carries the Paralyzed — 4
   Redeemed for Relationship — 6
   I Want Your Heart — 7
   My Unfailing Love for You — 8
   Hear My Voice — 10
   First Fruits — 11
   I See Your Weaknesses — 13
   Drop the Keys — 15
   My Love for You Never Ends — 16
   Faith that Takes the Risk — 18
   Yes, You Hear My Voice — 18
   Childlike Faith — 20
   Small Seed of Faith — 21
   You Wear My Signet Ring — 23
   Stay Close, Stay Cultivated to Receive — 24
   Glory Through Your Weariness — 26
   Speak Out for Me — 27
   Don't Be Surprised. I Chose You — 28
   You Now Have This Light — 30
   Trust Me In the Storm — 31
   Fully Clothed and Perfectly Sane — 32
   A New, Tender Heart — 34
   Hometown Unbelief — 35
   Praise that Breaks Through — 36
   Remain — 37
   As Much as You Can Understand — 39
   Stay Well-Watered — 40
   Preparing the Soil to Receive — 41
   You are My Lampstand — 42

Ken LaPoint

Keep Your Childlike Heart	*43*
Shine and Burn	*45*
How Will You Respond This Day?	*46*
Follow Me in Wisdom	*48*
A Firm Foundation Requires Excavation	*49*
My Glory Will Be Revealed	*50*
Storms tell more than Stories	*52*
Another Storm?	*53*
Stand and Believe	*54*
Blueprint of Love	*55*
Faith to Hold Course	*56*
Learn From the Children Around You	*58*
Be Careful How You Hear	*59*
I Still Am	*60*
Sent to Speak with Full Power	*62*
I Rejoice Over You	*62*
My Fullness Fully Dwells	*64*
Stand Firm, Soldier	*65*
Am I Your First Love?	*67*
My Words Are Forever	*68*
Turn Back to Your First Love	*69*
Buried Truth	*70*
Pressed On Every Side	*72*
Light That Overcomes	*73*
Stay Close and Listen	*74*
You are Well Built and Well Planned	*76*
Many Trials for a Little While	*77*
Gold Worth Mining	*78*
Listen for Me	*79*
Adopted to Full Inheritance	*81*
Free to Choose	*83*
No Strings Attached	*84*
Faith Refined	*85*
Turn Your Heart Toward Me	*86*
Mark Well the Path on Which You Came	*88*

Why I journal the journey   **90**

LOVE, DAD

I Never Fail to Love You

"How precious to me are your thoughts, God!
How vast is the sum of them!
Were I to count them,
they would outnumber the grains of sand—
when I awake, I am still with you."
Psalm 139:17-18 NIV

My child,
Earthly fathers do their best to fulfill their promises to their children. In their sincere love they do their best and yet they still fail so often.

Child, my love for you is much more than sincere. My love for you is *unfailing*. There is never even a moment that I fail to love you.

My love for you began before you were born. It began even before your parents were born. I have loved you since before I spoke the earth into existence. Yes, every day, every plan and every design I wrote about you, that I wrote for you, before I created the very first day, I have written in my very great love for you.

When hardship comes, my love doesn't fail. Don't let pain or struggle cause your heart to feel that my love for you has diminished. Unfailing love never fails to love.

My love for you is jealously protective and wise. My eye is always on you and my heart is always for you.

How I desire for you to know the depths of my love for you. When you walk on level, well-marked pathways along a tree-lined riverbank you can easily sense my love for you. When your path begins to climb up a less traveled and difficult trail, my love for you still is unfailing. Whether I called you to take this difficult and treacherous trail or if it is a result of your own decisions, my love for you is *still* unfailing.

Let my perfect love for you drive out fear. Let me replace your anger and frustration with my perfect peace.

The steepest and most difficult mountain trails possess the most glorious and powerful vistas. I may call you to walk trails so I can share the victory and the view from the mountain peak with you.

I am with you on every step of this journey. My love for you keeps me right beside you.

Even if you feel the path is the result of your disobedience, my love still will not fail to redeem your journey. My love for you is able to redeem you from the deepest pit.

Where I am, so is my love for you. Can we walk this day together? I will speak to you of my love all along the way. I am always thinking of you.

Precious child, my unfailing love will never fail to love you.

Love, Dad

Your Last Two Cents

"Jesus called his disciples to him and said, "I tell you the truth, this poor widow has given more than all the others who are making contributions. For they gave a tiny part of their surplus, but she, poor as she is, has give everything she had to live on." Mark 12:43-44

Faithful one,

All. When the poor widow gave that day, she gave her all. All her trust and all her faith she placed upon me.

How great was her heart of faith. Even though her journey had pain, loss and hardship her faith was completely on me. She had lost her husband. She had lost the love and care he gave her. She had been left a widow with nothing much to live on.

Her tithe that day was 100% of her heart of faith. As she placed those coins in the collection box, I heard her heart shout, "I love you, Daddy I trust you even more."

Child, rejoice. This is the heart I am searching for. This is the heart that will cause me to rush in and to fully support. I will rush into your loyalty. I will strengthen your loyal and trusting heart.

Your loyalty brings me glory. When your soul feels widowed and poor; when it feels like you've been striving for years; when you feel as if the love of your life has died and left you to fend for yourself... When your heart feels like you only have two cents worth of hope and your life demands much more, stay loyal to me. Stay faithful.

The widow could have turned away as she saw all the others put their large offerings in the collection box. She could have turned away feeling inferior, poor and with nothing to offer.

She could have held her last two cents of hope tightly in the fear of what she was going to do if she had $0.00 in her possession. Yet her loyal and trusting heart caught me attention as she walked up to that box. Even though her gift may have seemed very insignificant to anyone else, *it spoke volumes to the One to whom she gave it.*

I rejoice over those whose heart is 100% mine. I rush into the heart that puts their last two cents of hope in me. How blessed you are when your spirit is poor. You see me when you are poor in spirit. I open my heart and pour out heaven's riches upon yours. I will not hold back the riches of my love. I will not hold back the riches of my presence. I will not hold it back.

Some seek me when their life is full and they rejoice in giving me from the surplus of their heart.

But how precious is your gift when all but two cents of your hope has been spent and yet your loyal trusting heart gives me all you have left. Trust me to meet your full trust with my full heart of compassion.

Love, Dad

Faith that Carries the Paralyzed

Some people brought to him a paralyzed man on a mat. Seeing their faith, Jesus said to the paralyzed man, "Be encouraged, my child! Your sins are forgiven."
Matthew 9:2

Faithful child,
Your prayers of faith are what will carry the paralyzed into my presence. It took four men to carry their paralyzed friend to me; their friend who had been stuck; unable to move for thirty-eight years of his life. It was the loving faith of his four friends that carried him- just as he

was; stuck, paralyzed- with his mat.

Even when they saw how his mat and his condition appeared to be too big and cumbersome to fit into that crowded house, they didn't let up. They did not waiver in their faith. They knew they were going to get their paralyzed friend into my presence for a face-to-face encounter.

As they dug open the roof; as dirt and debris fell upon those all around me; they saw the looks of disapproval on the faces of the unsettled religious in the house. Yet their faith did not waiver.

What everyone else saw as a disturbance and an interruption, I saw as *life-changing* faith. Even the paralytic man was embarrassed and felt out of place. He couldn't do anything other than go along for the ride.

As I looked up at the four men, I saw their eyes filled with faith. Filled with confidence and trust!

Their faith moved them in love and yet in bold confidence and strength. These are the hearts that get my attention. This is the bold faith that creates a dust and debris storm as it breaks through the barriers to get to my presence.

This is the faith that lovingly carries a stuck, paralyzed one. Don't let your friend's unbelief keep you from carrying him into my presence.

Faithfulness to me and their loving faithfulness to their beloved friend had tremendous and life-changing power.

I am still looking for those who are faithful to break through for their friends.

Love, Dad

P.S. Did you know you're looking more and more like your Father every day?

Redeemed for Relationship

"At one time we thought of Christ merely from a human point of view. How differently we know him now. This means that anyone who belongs to Christ has become a new person. The old life has gone, a new life has begun." 2 Corinthians 5:16-18

"The name of the Lord is a fortified tower; the righteous run into it and are safe." Proverbs 18:10 NIV

Precious Child,

You have been redeemed with a great price and a great love. You are redeemed! Restored! I have pursued you for relationship. How great is my love for you! You are my prized creation. You are created for relationship with me!

Does a bridegroom court his bride with great passion just to say "I do" and then afterward expect his wife to live apart from him? Does he simply desire his bride to live and speak as if she is married and have no intimate personal, one-to-one relationship with him?

How his heart would be broken. He desires the marriage ceremony to be the announcement of the beginning of their ever-deepening, ever-closer relationship.

I have pursued you with my whole heart so I can be with you I desire you to know my very heart. So spend time with me each day and I will speak to your heart. . Isn't it true you know best those with whom you have spent the most time?

The sheep that have been with the shepherd the longest are the quickest to recognize his voice. They are the ones who respond swiftly to his call.

My Spirit resides in you. This is truly a foretaste

of heaven. I have put my very spirit in you-the most intimate of relationships! Open your heart to mine. Hear my voice calling. I have much to tell you. I have much to show you. There is so much to pour out to you. You are greatly loved! You are adopted! Not just rescued and made right-you are greatly loved, my child. I have rescued you for an ever-deepening relationship with me.

Love, Dad

I Want Your Heart

"Look! I stand at the door and knock. If you hear my voice and open the door, I will come in, and we will share a meal together as friends." Revelation 3:20

My adopted child,
 I desire for you to know my very heart. Religiosity may have studied my life, analyzing the scriptures, but my desire for you is much deeper, and so much more intimate.
 I have placed my very Spirit within your heart for you are my heart's desire.
 As you read my scriptures, do you see my love for you? Every word speaks of my love-for YOU. My spirit within you will guide your heart to an ever-deepening revelation of my love.
 I am a good husband. Does a good husband simply love his wife with all his mind? Just because he understands how to provide for her- even if he is a 'textbook' great man- this won't reach her heart.
 But a husband who opens his heart, sometimes at

the risk of an unreceptive response, is one that is a truly loving husband. How he desires to connect with the heart of his bride. When their hearts are one, his heart is filled with great, great joy.

He cannot demand unity and intimacy. No, it is earned by his love that he unselfishly has poured out. A good husband never gives up. He will pour out his love even when it falls on deaf ears and an unreceptive heart.

My love pursues you. I am after your heart. I want you to sense my intimate presence. I want you to fully experience what my heart holds. There is great compassion, joy and even sorrow.

As my Spirit reveals my heart to you, my written Scriptures will become more and more your favorite love song.

Let me share my heart with yours.

Love, Dad

My Unfailing Love for You

"LORD, give me your unfailing love, the salvation that you promised me." Psalm 119:41

Weary Child,
I desire to fill you so full with my Spirit and my presence that it overflows. I long to fill you with my love until it pours out from you in uncontrollable joy. There is no need to fear losing this love or any need to worry that this is a passing season. My love for you is truly unfailing. There is no end to my great love for you, dear

child.

My mercy toward you is truly tender. Child, you hold a very special place in my heart.

I have chosen your heart as the place for my spirit to dwell within you. There is so much I desire to pour out upon you and through you; more than your mind can begin to understand or explain. Yet your heart will *know* because your heart is where my Spirit resides.

As you have studied the Scriptures, you have understood my truths. Now my Spirit will draw you deeper into those truths. Watch how my Spirit breathes my love into what you have learned about me. Every one of my truths is wrapped within my great love for you.

I love you child. Why do you approach me as if you are approaching a border crossing to a foreign country? Children of the King are recognized as such and have full authority to be in the King's presence.

Child I recognize you as mine. Your passport has been stamped once and for all in my blood. So enter my presence with joy. Enter with praise. Enter expecting me.

So stay close. Stay faithful and attentive. I have much to show you. I have so much to share with you. There is so much in which I want you to share with me.

I could tell you everything in hopes that you will comprehend, but how much better to *experience* these things with me. As you step out in faith and take the risk to share what I pour out to you, your heart will know and will help your mind to understand as well.

My love for you is much bigger, deeper and powerful than your human mind could understand fully. Yet, my Spirit dwells in your heart and my Spirit is the revealer.

Just as the curtain to the Holy of Holies was torn open and revealed the heart of the temple to all who looked that direction, so my Spirit reveals my exposed heart of loving, tender mercy for you.

You cannot earn my love. You cannot measure up to my acceptance. Just your humble acceptance of my love will do. There is nothing you can provide to be accepted by me; you simply need to accept my loving provision for you.

Remember I tore the veil. I am the one who has made the way when there wasn't a way. I am opening my heart to you. I am the one who so desires for you to be with me.

Your heart will understand. Say yes to this father's heart!

Love, Dad

Hear My Voice

"For God says, "At the right time, I heard you…"
2 Corinthians 6:1

My precious child,

Just as the winds blow causing the trees to clap their hands in praise, so I desire the wind of my spirit to stir your heart to shout out praise to me. Yet also, how I desire for you to hear my voice! Do you think I am distant and far away? Do you think I am too busy to speak to you? Why do you live as if I only had just enough time, enough love for you to save you and then get you started in the right direction… and then I had to get back to work? Did you think I would be silent and leave you guessing?

Is that why you do not expect to hear me speak to you? My heart is full and I desire to share it fully with you. I have so much I desire to share with you, to show you and so much to experience with you.

Remember I can speak at any moment. Keep your ear tuned to hear me. How a shepherd loves to see his little lamb stop, lift his head and look at him at the very first sound of his shepherd's voice!

My heart's desire is that you recognize my voice as soon as I clear my voice to speak. Yet, don't get discouraged. Stay attentive. Keep listening. I will change your, "Is that you, Dad?" into "That *is* you, Dad!"

The more time you spend with me, the better you will know my voice. It is an ever-deepening process; so do not be discouraged if you miss it at first. Just like a baby first learns to sit, then crawl, then to stand and to walk… and one day to run so it is for you as you learn to hear my voice and my heart for you.

Just as a child's parent is right there with him from infancy to when he can run, so I am here with you. And just as that child will learn to quickly hear and recognize his parent's voice, so will you recognize mine.

I will not be silent. All the quiet moments your spend with me will make you quick to hear me. I love you.

Love, Dad

First Fruits

"And we believers also groan, even though we have the Holy Spirit with us as a foretaste of future glory."
Romans 8:23

Child,

You have a foretaste of future glory. Remember the parable of the three servants? How each was entrusted with one, two and five bags of silver? How each was called to give account for how they had added value to the "first fruits" the master had given them?

So it is with the first fruits of the Holy Spirit I have invested and entrusted to be in you. "To those who use well what they are given, even more will be given". (Matt 25:29). My promises are yes and amen. I rush to meet your risk-taking steps of faith. Watch how as you step out in faith your "risk-investment" will earn an increase.

I have come and given you a first-fruit box of my father's love for you. Look. The box is full and filled to overflowing. There is so much fresh, ripe, sweet and delicious fruit. There is too much to keep it all to yourself. If you do keep it all, it will spoil and be of very little value. So give it away. Watch how I will cause there to be miraculous increase.

My spirit within you is the first fruits I have given to you. So take the risk to give away what I have entrusted to you. Give away my words of love, my joy, the peace and confidence that fills your life.

You will find that your first-fruit box will never be depleted as you give it away. My mercies will always be new every day.

Your risk-taking faith that gives away your first fruits keep the flood of blessing flowing. Yet if you doubt, fear and bury it in the ground- hidden out of sight- what good is that? Why would I pour out more to someone who isn't using what I've already poured out to them?

To those who use well what they are given, even more will be given and they will have abundance.

Allow me to turn your doubt-filled questions into declarations of "Yes, I will take the risk and give away the first-fruits of Holy Spirit within me."

Remember I have entrusted Holy Spirit into your life. I know what you together with my spirit are capable to do. Remember, with me all things are truly possible.

All things. So take the full risk and see how sweet and satisfying are the first fruits that I have already given you. The first fruits of heaven are yours. I am not the harsh taskmaster of a boss that you have to keep from anger. No, I am your loving Father.

It brings me great joy to see my children taking full advantage of what I have given them.

My sheep know my voice. They know my call. They know my prompting. I will prompt your heart. Keep your ear attentive for my call and you will know the how's and when's and the who's I will call you to whom I call you to pour out my love, hope, encouragement and love.

More is waiting to be poured out to you. Give away what you've been entrusted and watch how swiftly I will refill, replenish and refresh you.

I am ready. Child are you?

Love, Dad

I See Your Weaknesses

"The Holy Spirit helps us in our weakness.."
Romans 8:26

Men look at the outward appearance, but I always look at your heart. My love chose you. I see your weaknesses and they don't change my love for you. When my spirit moves within you and when you follow my prompting I get glorified.

In your weakness, press into me. Did I not tell you I would use all things? Take notice of how your entire body has to respond when sickness comes upon you. Illness may cause you to slow down, to keep warm – even lie still in bed.

Allow me to speak into this time. Could it be that I've chosen to slow you down so that I can have your full attention? Could I not use what the enemy means to use as discouragement and derailment from your great plans as a tremendously powerful experience with me?

Let my spirit be strong in your weakness. I accept you with all your weaknesses. My acceptance should suffice. Don't be worried or concerned about other's interpretations of your weakness, or sickness. Remember they make their assessments based on what they see.

So let them see my glory even in your weakness. Yes, even in your time of sickness. The contrast of my glory being shown in the midst of your weakness is just like placing diamonds on a black velvet surface. Their magnificence and brilliance are enhanced as they are placed against the contrast of the blackened background. The black surface shows off their glory. Together, the velvet causes their glory to shine even more.

Let me have your weakness, your sickness. Watch how I will receive glory. Even in your weakness, your illness, I can be glorified.

My presence in your black-as-black-velvet-situation can change hopelessness into glory. Let my glory shine in you. If you let me, I can even change your weariness into a heart that sings, "Here is my black velvet ready for your glorious diamonds." I will always place my diamonds on your surrendered, black velvet situation. Let's shine today. You are so greatly loved.

Love, Dad

Drop the Keys

"God saved you by his grace when you believed. And you can't take credit for this; it is a gift from God. Salvation is not a reward for the good things we have done, so none of us can boast about it." Ephesians 2:8-9

My Child,
You cannot stand outside of my presence trying to figure out the right way to enter. It is as if you stand there with a big key ring full of keys. You hold a key of repentance, a key of humility- a key for everything.

Child, look at the door. It is wide open. My great love for you has opened the door. In fact, look at the door again. The lock is gone!

So put down your key ring of religiosity. I desire you to be with me. Let me exchange your key ring of religiosity for the signet ring of sonship. "You have not received a spirit that makes you a fearful slave" (Romans 8:15) to hold onto a keychain of religious requirements. No child, you have been adopted. You have been given full family sonship. How I love to hear you call me, "Dad".

That key ring was something you had to hang

onto. You had to be careful not to lose the keys that unlocked all the locks of religiosity. But my signet ring is securely on your hand. That is where it always will be. Now your hands are free. They are open to receive what I have to give you. I have given you my love. I adopted you into my family. And you have my glory.

I, your father am for you. I love you. I see your heart… and I love you. I see your struggles and failures… and I love you. Drop your keys; take my ring.

Love, Dad

My Love for You Never Ends

"Your treasure will be safe; no thief can steal it and no moth can destroy it. Where ever your treasure is, there the desires of your heart will also be." Luke 12:33-34

Child,
Don't sit outside on the steps of the "The Bank of the Treasures of Heaven" feeling lost, forgotten and poor. Remember whose child you are. The riches of heaven are open to you because you are my child.

There is nothing you could do to change your sonship. There is nothing that can change my great love that adopted you. You could sit on the steps stuck in your feeling unworthy and unaccepted, but the treasures of heaven are right inside. They are still waiting for you. So am I.

Why do you live as if you need to go collect bottles for redemption? My love for you is not based on your meager attempts at earning my approval. My love is my gift. Why do you feel as if you need to exchange your attempts for my approval and acceptance?

The only deposit you will ever need is my spirit who was deposited in you when I adopted you.

I am not after your performance; I'm after your heart. I don't want you doing things for me; what I desire is for you to do them *with* me. It's whose you are that matters. You are mine. Precious! Valuable! Already redeemed!

I know every detail about you. I know the number of hairs on your head- because I made you with great care and much thought- you are so precious to me and so valuable to me.

My heart is for you. It gives me great happiness to give you my kingdom. It gives me such joy when you accept the treasures of my kingdom. Why would I tell you to be giving and generous and then be a stingy miser with my own kingdom?

Look at a single tree. Try to count the leaves on just that one tree. There are so many. Have you lost count yet?

Now stand at the edge of a tree-covered hillside. Can you count all of the leaves on all the trees?

So is my love for you. So are the riches of the kingdom of heaven. Did you feel like it would take forever to count all the leaves on all those trees? That is how I want you to understand my love for you. It will go on forever. The more you count, the more there is to count. There is no end to the depth of my love for you, my child.

Love, Dad

Faith that Takes the Risk

" Anyone who wants to come to him must believe that God exists and that he rewards those who sincerely seek him." Hebrews 11:6b

My Child,
Yes, my spirit has been a gift to you. Will you open that gift today? Open it and see how my spirit will marry yours and together we will change lives.

Don't doubt it. Don't fear it. Enjoy what we will do. Don't hesitate. I am with you. You carry my name. You walk in my authority.

Take the risk instead of wondering! Trust my spirit who is speaking to your heart. Watch how I rush in to pour my love into your faith-filled attempt.

You will do greater things- just trust. Just listen and step out. I love you and I am proud of your listening heart and childlike faith. I, your father am filled with joy when you walk in my footsteps.

Are you ready? Let's go.

Love, Dad

Yes, You Hear My Voice

"These words you hear are not my own; they belong to the Father who sent me." John 14:24 NIV

Sweet child of mine,
Yes, you are hearing my heart speak to yours. Did I not promise to open deaf ears? The ears of your

heart have been opened.

Now, with just a word- just a word from my lips can capture your attention. When I speak, I see you gaze upon me and it brings me joy. Your love for me is showing more and more.

When I have the attention of your heart, I will speak to you. I have been searching for hearts such as yours.

I can speak to an attentive heart. You yourself know what it's like to lose someone's attention as you are speaking to him; you stop talking because you know they are not listening to you. Why waste your words when ears have been deafened to your voice? Yet when I have your faith-filled attention, I will share my deepest thoughts with you.

Do you feel unworthy? Do you feel that your prodigal wandering and disobedience have disqualified you? Child, let my love wash you free of any remnant or smell of the pig food in which you had been living. Let my love gently cleanse you free of guilt and restore you to full sonship.

There is no need to feel substandard- as if you are only worthy of being an employee. I have restored you to full *sonship*. I want to celebrate with you today. I rejoice because you are mine! I have been waiting for this day to tell you all that has been on my heart.

I am the one who paid all the cost. It has already been paid in full. The table is set. The celebration meal is ready to be served. The robe of your sonship is waiting for you as well.

Remember how Moses' face shone after being in the presence of my glory? Remember how others couldn't help but notice how I had changed him? So shall my glory change you. Others will see my glory in you and give me praise.

As they do, their desire to experience my glorious presence will increase.

So come. Listen. Partake with me. Your listening heart is as a key in a padlock on the doors of my presence and blessing. No longer will the doors hold back the mighty flowing river of my presence.

Get ready for my joy and refreshment to wash over you.

Love, Dad

Childlike Faith

"When Jesus saw what was happening, he was angry with his disciples. He said to them, "Let the children come to me. Don't stop them! For the Kingdom of God belongs to those who are like these children." Mark 10:14

Sweet child,

Your childlike faith, your childlike trust, your childlike obedience stirs my heart. When you do what I ask of you, my heart smiles with joy.

A childlike heart will not need me to explain. The heart of a child takes me at my word in full. It trusts and knows I will not ever mislead him. He needs no explanation because he trusts daddy 100%. He will fully comprehend- not because I explained it first- but because he experienced Daddy's word being true as he obeyed.

Daddy's word was proven in his childlike obedience. He simply trusted and obeyed. "How blessed you will be as you trust me without seeing (John 20:29).

A child will trust and believe without seeing

because his daddy is his hero. His daddy is loving. Dad wouldn't tell him to do something silly or hurtful. But I see *your* doubt.

Earthly fathers often fail and disappoint; yet I am your Heavenly Father. I will not leave you. I will not forsake you. I am worthy of your trust and obedience.

The failure of earthly dads has hardened the hearts of their children. Their childlike faith gets discarded as if it were foolishness. Childlike faith opens heaven upon you.

How it saddens me to see the example of closed and hardened hearts passed from one generation to the next. Claim my tender mercy that will set your imprisoned heart free.

A child will accept a gift no matter how big or how small. He accepts it with great joy. Yet many adults seem the think they need to reciprocate when someone gives a gift to them. They often feel an obligation to give something in return.

You are my child. How great is my joy just to see your joyous excitement as I pour out my extravagant love upon your receptive, childlike heart. Accept my gift with a child's trusting heart. Claim my gifts of my promises and unfailing love. Let me love you. This makes *my* joy full.

Love, Dad

Small Seed of Faith

"How blessed are those who are hungry and thirsty for righteousness, because it is they who will be satisfied!" Matthew 5:6

Sweet Child,

Do you look down the road, anxiously waiting? Do you feel I am distant? Do you even wonder if I'm heading your direction?

Look. I am standing right beside you. I have been here all along.

Let your childlike faith allow your eyes to open. Let your heart hear my voice once again. How it delights me to give you the treasures of heaven. When your eyes are opened and your ears hear my voice, I will not hold back.

The floodgates of my love shall explode over you. But don't be afraid, little lamb. The flood is my pure love. Let it wash away your loneliness and sorrow.

Even the tiniest, mustard-seed-sized grain of faith shall burst forth into enormously oversized trees of blessing.

Give me that one little seed of faith. That is all I need. Just the one! I will cause it to burst into the tallest tree.

Little child, when your faith is small and I seem miles away from you, just turn toward me. Drop your tiny seed of faith in my hand. I will rush in. The floodgates of my loving presence cannot hold back any longer.

Isn't this what your heart is dying for? Isn't this what I died to give to you?

Make my heart glad,

Love, Dad

You Wear My Signet Ring

"The people were amazed at his teaching, for he taught with real authority- quite unlike the teachers of religious law." Mark 1:22

Dear Child,

You wear my signet ring on your right hand. You carry full authority- my full authority. My child, whom I love, you need to know that heavenly realms recognize the authority that my signet ring contains.

Remember that a lamp is not meant to be hidden. It shines for all to see. Its light is meant to cancel the darkness and expose hidden things.

So why do you keep your hand in your pocket? Why do you hide the glory of my signet ring I placed upon your hand?

Holy Spirit is my signet ring upon your life. Angels shout with joy in the presence of Holy Spirit upon you. Demons tremble in terror as well for they fully know the one wearing my authority, my ring, and my very spirit, can destroy them and their schemes.

I have placed Holy Spirit, my signet ring on you to be visible to others. Does a bride hide here wedding ring from view? No. She wears it proudly to show all that she is greatly loved. She wants all to know how much her husband loves her.

So shine and let all know how much I love you. Let Holy Spirit be visible and no longer hidden.

When you take the risk, my authority I give you will be apparent. The enemy wants you to keep your authority hidden deep in your pocket in fear of failure.

Yet it is my Spirit and my promises to you will never fail. My love for you will never fail. Nor will the authority Holy Spirit carries ever fail you.

The prodigal son was humbled as his dad put his signet ring on his finger. His feelings of unworthiness to receive it just made his father love him even more.

I, your father, will put my ring on your hand. I will wipe away your repentant tears and hold your hand high for all to see. I rejoice because you are my child. You have my ring. I rejoice over you. Let me hold your hand high!

Not just a servant, you are my child. Wear my ring that carries my authority. It will be honored. It is the light that overcomes darkness. Do not fear to do my bidding- ever.

I love you,
Dad

P.S.

The need for torches of light- even in places where the light previously had shone- is desperate. The light of my love overcomes darkness, fear and discouragement. My light overcomes any darkness.

When has darkness ever consumed the light? I have ignited your heart. What can you do but shine? What can you do but burn brightly?

Stay Close, Stay Cultivated to Receive

"Still other seeds fell on fertile soil, and they sprouted, grew, and produced a crop that was thirty, sixty, and even a hundred times as much as had been planted!" Mark 4:8

Dear Child,

When I have your heart fully- when I have your full attention I will open my heart to you with great intention.

My thoughts are always for you. You are my young lamb. Even though my flock is great in number, I keep my eye upon you. Stay close to my and you will learn to quickly recognize my call. You will be able to distinguish my voice from all others.

Your attentive heart will quickly recognize my loving presence. It is like fertile soil ready to receive seeds I desire to plant in your very heart and soul.

I am a very intentional farmer. I plant seeds for a harvest and I also plant seed that will bring me joy.

The same farmer who plants row upon row of corn can also plant seeds that burst forth with flowers; flowers that bring bright colors to stand out in great contrast to the abundance of green stalks.

Stay tenderhearted and attentive so the soil of your heart is always ready to receive that which I desire to plant in you.

There isn't any type of soil I cannot cultivate and amend to become rich and fertile. I am the good farmer. I am the loving farmer. I can remove even the most stubborn of rocks in the soil of your heart. I can break up the most hardened pathways of habit. There is no soil that is a lost cause.

Let me redeem that which you consider as hopeless. Trust me. My heart is for you. I know the beauty and growth I can create in you.

Stay close to me today.

Love, Dad

Glory Through Your Weariness

"Then Jesus said, "Come to me, all of you who are weary and carry heavy burdens, and I will give you rest." Matthew 11:28

Weary Child,
Let me revive you today. My mercies are reviving and new every morning. I see your weariness from attempting to carry your heavy load of responsibilities and concerns- yes I see your worries too.

I so desire to revive you. Yet I see you awaken, get ready for the day, and with great intention, soar off to take care of your day's 'laundry list'.

Come to me with your burden of worries and responsibilities. Rest is waiting for you. You let your body rest each night as you lay in bed; you recharge your phone as you plug it into its charger. How I desire to recharge your soul as your spend time with me.

Does it sound as if I am asking you to take on 'just another responsibility'? Does your heart say, "Now I have to spend time with Jesus because I want him to be proud of me."?

Oh child, set that lie from the enemy aside. "You have not received a spirit that makes you fearful slaves. Instead you have received my spirit when I adopted you as my own." (Romans 8:15) I adopted you because I love you and cannot stand the thought of being apart from you.

Every morning, I am waiting for you. My heart is bursting with love for you. I have put my spirit within your very soul because I want the closest possible relationship with you.

Let's do life together today. Let me share the

deepest parts of my heart with yours. You are my adopted one and I love you.

Love, Dad

Speak Out for Me

"For God has not given us a spirit of fear and timidity, but of power, love, and self-discipline."
2 Timothy 1:7

Child,

I did not place my spirit within you to remain secretive and silent. I speak to your heart so that you will speak for me.

Your time with me has caused you to hear and to recognize my voice. You know what my voice sounds like. You know when I call you. You recognize the phrases I use, the inflections of my spirit's voice. You know what my heart speaks to yours.

So as we go through this day, with its many voices calling for your attention, keep your heart attuned to hear my call. Be ready to speak my words of encouragement, comfort and strength.

Every word I speak has great power. I have opened my heart to yours. As I speak to your heart, now open your mouth and speak my heart over those you encounter today.

Pour out my powerful words of encouragement over those who are stuck in discouragement. As you speak, my words will renew their faith.

So trust me in that exact moment. It is time to move past your thoughts of, "Is that you Lord asking me to speak for you?" and say "Yes, Lord. I will speak for you."

Your heart holds the greatest treasure- my very spirit. Your clay-jar life may feel unworthy to carry such a valuable treasure, but my glory shines in your humble and obedient heart as brilliantly as diamonds shine when they are placed on a black velvet cloth.

Speak my heart. Trust my voice and speak over the weak. Do my bidding. My words will strengthen them.

Trust me to speak. Be quick to hear me. Take the risk to speak for me. My words hold power. My words are the words that hold power-not yours.

Your faith to trust me and to speak for me will pour out power-filled love. It will pour out power-filled strength. It will pour out power-filled comfort and encouragement.

I can do power-filled things with you as you trust my voice and use yours.

Love, Dad

Don't Be Surprised. I Chose You

"When Jesus heard this, he told them, 'Healthy people don't need a doctor- sick people do. I have come to call not those who think they are righteous, but those who know they are sinners.' Mark 2:17

Dear Child,
Are you surprised that I have chosen to put my power and gifts within you? You received my power

when the Holy Spirit came upon you. (Acts 1:8)

How I desire to show my power in you! How I desire my power to be strongly evident in your life. Why would I give you Holy Spirit's power if I didn't want you to bring me glory today?

When you were baptized with water, you were fully immersed and surrounded in the water. So it is with my spirit. You are fully immersed and fully surrounded. How great is my love for you. Don't allow your feelings of unworthiness stop you at the bank of my baptizing river. Do you feel as if you are only worthy to come close enough to fill a your cup?

Take my hand and step into the water. Come out into deeper water. Child, I myself want to baptize you. I am the one who holds you securely as I fully immerse you in my Spirit. Fully immersed in my presence. Fully immersed and held very securely. Fully washed over by my Spirit. Fully immersed in my power.

I have given you Holy Spirit's power and I give you authority to use that power. I see your hesitance to step out in my authority. I am with you always. My authorization shall always be honored. My presence with you will cause my authority in you to be honored and respected. You have received my power and authority.

Keep close to me today for I desire to touch lives through the power I have place within you. I will prompt your heart to speak my words of life, love, encouragement, and faith. Speak my power-filled words. Don't keep them contained only in your thoughts.

I will prompt you to take action today that will release my power. Stay close beside me. Don't miss this.

Just as a lamp lights up a whole room and all benefit from its illumination, so will you be energized in your giving away of my power. You will be re-filled with joy. Your faith will be power-filled. I will heighten your awareness of my presence.

So stay close to me today. You are filled. You are empowered. And you are authorized.

Give me glory today.

Love, Dad

You Now Have This Light

"We now have this light shining in our hearts…"
2 Corinthians. 4:7

My adopted one,

What part of *"now"* don't your understand? I desire to make my glory evident in you. I desire that my great power be evident in you.

You *now* have this great treasure in your very heart. It is my treasure that shines- not your fragile clay jar. Your attempts to clean up your little clay jar only distract those that need to see my glory- my treasure that you carry.

Take me at my promise to you. You *now* hold this great treasure. You have my very spirit dwelling in you. My promise is my promise. I am always true to my word.

When you heard me knocking, you opened the door and I came fully and completely in. Why do you live as if I had said, "Behold I stand at the door and knock. If you open the door and if your house is clean, neat and meets my white glove standards, then I'll come in"?

When you opened the door, I saw you, my child

for whom I paid the highest price. I paid that price so I could be with you. When you opened the door of your heart to me, I came rushing in.

You, like so many, look at the outward appearance and wonder, "What could God ever do with my confused and messy life?" But I see your heart. My presence makes all things new.

You have my light shining in your heart. I will make it clear this is my great power and it will be evident it is my power within you.

My glory and power shines in you- because it is *my* glory and power. You are already adopted into the fullest of sonship because I paid so high a price to redeem you.

You *now* have this light, this great treasure and it shows my power and brings me glory. I will shine brightly in you, my fragile clay jar!

Love, Dad

Trust Me In the Storm

"So be strong and courageous! Do not be afraid and do not panic before them. For the LORD your God will personally go ahead of you. He will neither fail you nor abandon you." Deuteronomy 31:6

My chosen child,
When storms come, the wind and waves that arise will certainly get your attention. The enemy will misuse them to create fear and anger in your heart. How he wants you to forget I am with you. Child, he wants you to rush to take control of your sailing ship and head out of the storm quickly and to take the most direct route out

of the storm.

Instead, will you trust me? Will you wait on me? Will you trust me in the midst of trouble? Why do you panic as if the storm has tossed me overboard and you have been left to fend for yourself?

I will never leave your side. I will never forsake you. Your panic and rash attempts to remedy the situation on your own won't bring my peace. My peace passes your abilities. My peace *calms* the storm.

Heading back to where you came from may bring you to a calm place, but the storm still rages. You also have turned your ship in a direction I did not ask you to go.

Trust me to keep you safe. Trust me to keep your heart on course. Trust me to calm your storm just as miraculously as I caused peace to rule over the disciples' storm that night on the Galilean Sea.

This storm will pass. I will always have control. On the other side of this, your faith will gain new strength and confidence to face storms such as this one.

Others will see your faith in me and your faith will change them. Your faith will strengthen their faith. Your faith will give them courage.

Trust me, my dear child. I will keep you on course even through storms such as this. I will bring peace and I will calm this storm.

Love, Dad

Fully Clothed and Perfectly Sane

"And a crowd soon gathered around Jesus and they

saw the man who had been possessed by the legion of demons. He was sitting there fully clothed and perfectly sane and they were afraid." Mark 5:15

Yes Child,

This once demon-possessed man sat fully clothed and perfectly sane in my presence. I changed his turmoil into sanity and peace.

When my disciples feared for their lives on that previous stormy night, they wanted me to deliver them *away* from the torment.

The townspeople of Gerasenes chained the demoniac out in a graveyard to keep their "storm" far *away* from them.

My peace passes your logic. My compassion will surprise you. Sit in my presence, just as this man did- fully clothed and perfectly sane. Fully clothed in my presence and in my power. My peace passes your logic; it passes your hope to be removed from your situation. I will pass it all to get to your heart. I will fully clothe your heart with my peace, presence and power.

Even though this now sane and fully clothed man begged me to take him away from his surroundings, I needed him to remain where he was. My peace had so radically transformed him that ten towns around him were never the same again.

Child, trust me to fully clothe you and keep you perfectly sane. Your transformed life may cause some to be fearful. It may cause some to want to be far removed from you. But trust me that your peace-filled, transformed life is affecting your ten surrounding towns.

You are in the right place, right now- fully clothed and perfectly sane by my Spirit. Power-filled peace changes and repurposes your storm. My peace passes your ability to explain, but when you experience it, everyone around you is affected by how my peace is evident in you.

Some will be afraid. Some will want to distance themselves from you. But do not lose sight of the ten towns that will be radically changed because you were radically changed.

Love, Dad

A New, Tender Heart

"And I will give you a new heart, and I will put a new spirit in you. I will take out your stony, stubborn heart and give you a tender, responsive heart." Ezekiel 36:26

My Child,

Trust me to be the loving surgeon that transplants a tender, responsive heart in place of your stony, stubborn and calloused one.

I am fully aware of how your stony heart has failed you. Let me give you *my new heart*. *Your* old stony heart cannot respond to my life-blood I desire to transfuse into you. Let me give you a new, tender, life-carrying heart. A new heart that brings my new life

Let my new heart carry new life to all of your soul. Let me pump my regenerating power into all parts of who you are. My new heart will turn your wastelands into a life-filled Garden of Eden.

Child, my heart's desire is to give you *my* heart.

Renew your mind! I desire to *give* you this new tender heart. A gift doesn't require repayment nor can it be earned. A gift needs only to be accepted. So accept this love-gift of my new heart; a tender, new, life-filled heart.

The old has gone; the new has come. (2 Corinthians 5:17)

How I want your heart to understand my heart. What better way than for you to have a tender new one. Let its life-blood revive, renew and regenerate all of your soul.

Your new heart will know mine as never before.

Love, Dad

Hometown Unbelief

"And because of their unbelief, He couldn't do any miracles among them except to place his hands on a few sick people and heal them. And He was amazed at their unbelief." Mark 6:5-6

Unbelief keeps the heart's door closed to spiritual. My own townspeople did not believe. Their disbelief closed the door to the spiritual and the supernatural. Their atmosphere of unbelief, doubting, and needing logical explanations was a spiritual atmosphere of its own. Their spirit of "No." closed the door of their hearts.

I stand at your door, knocking. I am standing at your door that the spirit of "No." desires to keep tightly closed.

This is one door your childlike faith can open. If you have forgotten what childlike faith looks like, I will remind you. Take special notice of every child that is near you today. Watch how they live in simple faith and childlike trust in the parents.

I am your loving father. Your logic cannot explain how the earth stays on course, yet you believe me. Your logic cannot explain the depths of the universe, yet you believe me.

So don't let your hometown logic keep you from believing that your father is spirit and wants to heal and change your atmosphere of "no" into a place where heaven is made manifest.

Say "Yes." in childlike faith. With me, all things are possible- all things.

Love, Dad

Praise that Breaks Through

"When the people heard the sound of the rams' horns, they shouted as loud as they could. Suddenly, the walls of Jericho collapsed, and the Israelites charged straight into the town and captured it." Joshua 6:20

Dear child,
Let me have your heart early before the volume of the world's voices begins to crash over you in overwhelming waves.

Arise early and turn your affection toward me. Open your heart to me before you put on the day's armor in preparation for today's battles. Let my perfect love cast out all of your fear.

Shouts of praise from obedient hearts destroyed the

fortified city of Jericho. The city was overtaken and conquered with shouts of praise. The walls of man's protection were no match for hearts filled with praise.

Turn your heart to me early and I will empower your praises. My powerful presence dwells in the praises of my children. "Didn't I tell you that you would see my glory if your believe?" (John 11:40)

Turn your heart toward me and sing my praises. I truly inhabit your praises. The fortified walls surrounding *your* heart are no contest for my power-filled presence.

Oh, did you think the "walls" were around other cities? The battles you face in life?

Child, the first fortified city is your own heart. Your walls will be dismantled by praise. Sing your praises. Affirm your trust in me. Your fortified city will crumble, and the gold and silver within you will I keep and treasure.

The strongholds of sin collapse as I empower your heart filled with praise! I will strengthen your faith as you see the walls of your "Jericho" give way to my love and power. Your praise and my presence unlock the victory over your Jericho and give your strength to face this day's battles.

Sing, my child, sing!

Love, Dad

Remain

"Remain in me and I will remain in you. For a branch cannot produce fruit if it is severed from the vine and you cannot be fruitful unless you remain in me.

Yes, I am the vine; you are the branches. Those who remain in me and I in them will produce much fruit. For apart from me you can do nothing." John 15:4-6

Precious one,

Stay with me even after all others have left your side for I have things yet to pour out to you. Stay with me. Remain with me. As you remain, I will reveal. I will reveal myself to you. I will reveal my heart to you.

There are those who you call friend, yet they are mere acquaintances. They recognize you. They greet you by name. Yet I am more that these.

There are others who are your dearest brothers. They come to your aid; they genuinely love you. You can confide in them, trust them with your troubles and joys. Yet, I am still more than these.

Your family is some of the closest to you. They know your shortcomings as well as your victories. They will stand for you and the family name more than any of your friends could possibly do. Yet I am still more than this.

I am your bridegroom. I desire to open the deepest parts of my heat to you. I desire to pour out the desires of my heart upon yours.

Stay with me after all others have left your side for I desire to pour out, lavish upon you, reveal to you, confide in you as a bridegroom confides in his beloved bride. I will reveal my heart.

Stay with me, remain with me for I have yet more to reveal to your heart. Remain expectantly. Yes, your joy will overflow.

Love, Dad

As Much as You Can Understand

"Jesus used many similar stories and illustrations to teach as much as they could understand." Mark 4:33

My Child,

As much as you can understand! As much as your heart can hold! As much as your arms can carry! I will pour out understanding upon you.

My heart's desire is that your heart beats in unison with mine. My heart beats in unison with the kingdom of heaven. Yes, my heartbeat is the heartbeat of heaven.

I want to open your heart, soul and mind to all of heaven's glory. Let your childlike faith arise.

Remember the little praise song, "Deep and wide, deep and wide, there's a fountain flowing deep and wide…?" There is no fountain of love deeper than my love for you. I will open wide my heart to you because I want you to understand. I want you to *know*.

One could tell you all about the excitement of mountain rock climbing. They could describe in vivid detail and passion filled emotion what rock climbing is like hoping that you catch their fire.

They could show you videos set to powerful music; they could even take you to the edge of the mountain cliff to show you what it's like. But all their attempts would fall short of putting you into a rock climbing harness and allowing you into the real life experience.

Then you understand; that's when you truly *know*.

That's how passionate I am about pouring out my kingdom to you. I am taking you to *experience* my glory, my love and my presence. Then you will truly know me; you will truly understand.

This is the intimacy I desire with you- as deep and as wide as you can handle.

Love, Dad

Stay Well-Watered

"The seed that fell in rocky soil represents those who hear the message and receive it with joy. But since they don't have deep roots they don't last long."

Mark 4:16-17

Dear One,
Stay firmly planted by my streams of living water. Allow your roots to grow deep and strong. Keep the promises of my inspired written word ever before you.

A well-established tree always starts from a tiny seed. A small seed can only grow into a well-established fruit-bearing tree if it remains in fertile soil and is well-watered.

Keep my promises before you. Meditate on them. Let me write them on the tablet of your heart. Let me saturate the soil of your heart with the water of my written word. Spend time in my presence.

Be deliberate and wait on me. Keep yourself planted by my streams of life-giving water. Well-watered means well-established.

A well-established root system brings life to every limb, every branch and every leaf of your life.

Spend time with me each day. Let the soil of your heart be saturated with the life-giving water of my Spirit.

Keep my promises ever before you. Let the life-giving Spirit produce much fruit on every branch of your life. Your abundant fruit will give life to others as well.

Keep my promises ever before you. Even the tallest of trees needs to remain well-watered or its leaves wither and fall.

Stay planted by my stream of living water and its life-giving water will bring life to every limb, every leaf!

What began as a seed is turning into a well-established tree that brings me glory.

Love, Dad

Preparing the Soil to Receive

"The seeds that fell among the thorns represents others who hear God's word, but all to quickly the message is crowed out by the worries of this life, the lure of wealth and the desire for other things, so no fruit is produced." Mark 4:18-19

My Child,

Consider the wise farmer. He takes time to prepare the soil of his fields before he plants. The wise farmer knows proper cultivation and soil preparation will bless him with a bountiful harvest.

He knows if he fails to put the plow into the soil, the ground will harden. Any seed that is sown upon hardened soil is merely bird food.

The intention of the farmer is planting for *abundance* so his soil must be properly prepared to receive. Seeds drop easily and remain secure in soil that has been made ready.

Child, my adopted one, the worries, desires and lures of this world will harden the soil of your heart. Stay close to me and I will keep your heart well-cultivated and always ready to receive!

I am the wise farmer. I keep a watchful eye upon you. My heart is for the field of your heart to see, to experience the joy of an abundant harvest with *your* heart.

I will even thwart the enemy's digging attempts to steal what has been planted within you. Trust me to turn his painful digging into my cultivation. Keep your eyes upon me.

Let me deeply cultivate the soil of your heart. There will be a harvest- a harvest in abundance! Your abundance will bless you and your family. There will be even sufficient blessing for the birds that perch in your branches and attempt to steal your harvest.

Remain close; stay deeply cultivated. Trust me for abundance.

Love,
Dad

You are My Lampstand

"A lamp is placed on a stand, where it will shine."
Mark 4:21

Child,
You are my lampstand where I choose to place my Spirit.

A lampstand by itself is of minimum value. Yet when a light is placed upon it, its glory shines and fills the room!

A lamp shines brightest in the darkest of surroundings. Where its light is most needed is exactly where its glory is most brilliantly evident.

But what good is a lamp that is lit and kept in the sunlight? A lamp is lit to dispel darkness. A burning flame's glory is revealed and darkness flees!

Take me at my word. Claim my promise. Don't fear if I ask you to bring my light into a darkened place. Light always shines and darkness always has to surrender to its glory. Trust me to shine in the darkest of places.

I promise to illuminate! That which was hidden will be plainly exposed. When you carry my light into dark places, everything is exposed. Even good things that had remained hidden in the darkness are brought out for all to see.

You are my lampstand in which I choose to put the glorious light of my Spirit. My heart's desire is for you to know the glory of carrying my light and my love to those lost in the darkness.

I promise to always shine!

Love,
Dad

Keep Your Childlike Heart

"When Jesus saw what was happening he was angry with his disciples. He said to them, "Let the children come to me! Don't stop them! For the Kingdom of God belongs to those who are like these children. I tell you the truth, anyone who doesn't receive the kingdom of

God like a child will never enter it." Mark 10:14-15

My Little One,

The Kingdom of God already belongs to those with simple, childlike faith. The heart of a child is sweet and trusting! A child simply loves to be with his father! Are you without a childlike heart? Where has your wonder gone?

Keep your heart of a child. Keep your wonder! Keep your joy!

The day that my disciples scolded parents for bringing their precious little ones to me was the day they began to lose sight of their own childlike heart!

The gates of my Kingdom stay open to the childlike. I pour out heaven's riches upon them.

Those with a child's heart are the ones I pull close in my arms. They are the ones I will bless with a touch of my presence!

A child will accept what daddy tells him without doubting. He will go wherever daddy says to go- without hesitation. He will do exactly what daddy asks him to do because he knows daddy's heart is always for him. He trusts daddy because he knows daddy loves him dearly!

When that child goes where daddy asks him, he finds the blessing waiting that his father promised. When he obeys his daddy's request to do something he will find his father's promises are *true*.

I am your loving daddy! How I long to open the Kingdom to you this very day! Will you trust me like a child who wholeheartedly trusts his daddy? Take me at my promises! This is so very simple even a child can understand this. Let simple childlike faith arise within you.

This cannot be contained or explained in a religious

formula. Using a pattern that worked for you before cannot approach it. It's trust! It's relationship with me. Like a father with his child! It's alive and creative!

Don't overlook it. The riches of relationship are open to those who simply accept my love with simple, child-hearted trust!

Your heavenly daddy is always true to his promises. My love for you never ceases.

Love, Dad

Shine and Burn

"You are the light of the world--like a city on a hilltop that cannot be hidden." Matthew 5:14

When a candle is ignited, it will burn and it will shine. The candle's creator fashioned it with full intention for it to burn strong and shine brightly. He carefully designed it to be a burner! It is intended to be a shiner! When he places a flame to the wick, it cannot do anything but catch the fire!

Let me ignite the wick of your spirit with the flame of my very spirit. I have fashioned you and designed your life to burn with intensity of the fire of my spirit! You spirit is set aflame when you say yes to me.

The flame of my spirit does not need a protective windscreen, but thrives in the winds of faith. I will empower the heat of your flame and the brilliance of it's shining as you step out in the winds of faith.

Burn with intensity, passion and love! Shine with intense passion and joy! Let my spirit turn your burning

candle into my lighthouse that gives direction to those who have lost their bearings. Let me turn your flame into a beacon that points them to the safety of my love and restores their hope.
    Burn and shine!

Love, Dad

How Will You Respond This Day?

"We now have this light shining in our hearts, but we ourselves are like fragile clay jars containing this great treasure. This makes it clear that our great power is from God, not from ourselves."   2 Corinthians 4:7

Child,
    You carry such incredibly priceless treasure! The fullness of the riches of heaven- the fullness of my presence! I have placed my spirit within you. Yet it wasn't for lack of a place to store it. I created order and purpose throughout the heavens and in all the earth. All creation shouts my glory and praise.
    I created you, my dear child, with great order and purpose. I have desired for you to be one with me. I want you to know my very heart. All creation shouts my glory and praise while at the same time it is my love song to you!
    My great mercy saved you. I showed mercy upon your sinful, perishing life because I love you. My design and purpose for you has always been to be more than just a carrier. My design is that you would be a responder to my love for you!

How desperate is the need for the lost and broken ones in the world around you to know and experience my love! Without my love, this world is just noise to those who are lost. Without my love they don't have reason to live in hope. Without my love the broken will just remain broken.

How will your heart reply to my presence this very day? All of creation is designed to shout my glory, yet I have given you, my child, the gift of choice. You have the choice to respond to my love.

All the rest of creation functions the way I created them to function, but to you, I gave a choice, a will- a free will. Without that free choice, love doesn't exist.

I chose to create all of the heavens and the earth. I chose to create the day and nighttime. I chose to fill the earth. I chose to fill it with life-giving water, snow-covered mountains, green fertile valleys and multitudes of animals. I prepared it all so it would be ready for you. I took dust from the ground and formed you in the midst of my prepared place for you. And when I had prepared you, I breathed my very life into you!

I planted the garden in Eden for you. When I placed a tree in which you were forbidden to partake, I gave you the power to choose. I imparted to you choice to love me and to trust me.

I chose to create the abundance of the heavens and the glory-filled earth to shout my praise but to also shout my great love for you!

How will your heart respond to my mercy and love today? How will you use the breath of my life that I have breathed into you? I love you and the choice is yours.

Love, Dad

Follow Me in Wisdom

"Wisdom is shown to be right by the lives of those that follow it." Luke 7:35

Precious One,
    As you walk where I am taking you, some may not understand. But follow me always. Walk with me no matter what may come. I am love. Always walk in compassion and love. I am light. Stay close to me for I am the light upon your pathway. I will always shine.
    Yes, heavenly wisdom proves how right it is when you faithfully follow. The path of heavenly wisdom is marked with the signposts of love, compassion, mercy and perseverance.
    Just as the religious experts of my day were blind to my wisdom and rejected it, so will you encounter those that do not understand. Even some will oppose you.
    You life is a signpost for those who oppose you. My wisdom will be shown to them as you follow me. Your life will expose them to my truth, my love and especially my wisdom.
    Stay close to my side. Seek my face before anything else.
    I will show my wisdom as you faithfully walk with me. Seek my face every day. Let me speak to you every day so my voice always is fresh in your mind and heart.
    Your faithfulness and your light will burn strong- it will show my wisdom. My wisdom is sure and is not tossed back and forth by stormy waves.
    Don't be afraid, I am here." (John 5:21)

Love, Dad

Love, Dad

A Firm Foundation Requires Excavation

"Anyone who listens to my teaching and follows it is wise, like a person who builds a house on solid rock. Though the rain comes in torrents and the floodwaters rise and the winds beat against that house, it won't collapse because it is built on bedrock."

Matthew 7: 24-25

Child,

The foundation I will build upon is formed as you listen to me. I am an intentional builder. Trust me during the times of excavation.

The base for your life is firmly established upon the solid and secure bedrock of my promises, salvation and my compassionate love for you.

Your foundation must be firmly rooted because the storms will come! Floodwaters will rise and fierce winds will threaten you. If life was without storms, a house could be built upon simple sand and without a foundation.

But a foundation rightly placed and firmly established allows me to build a structure that will last. It can stand as a legacy to be passed on to the generations to come.

I always excavate with love. I will remove loose, unstable soil and stubborn rocks to make sure your foundation is securely placed on the bedrock of my promises and truth.

Do not mistake the storm's rain and powerful wind's opposition as further excavation. The construction of your life-structure has been firmly established on the bedrock of our relationship. In my wisdom your foundation has been laid. It has been shaped with great purpose.

I am your loving father and I hold the blueprints of your life. A wise architect knows what type of foundation is required to sustain the structure of a lighthouse. He knows also, what type of foundations is required to hold a high-rise building in its place.

I am your wise and loving father and the foundation I have laid is exactly what is needed for what I am building upon it.

You are the structure I desire to build and you are a structure designed with great intention. You are a lighthouse upon a firm foundation and will weather heavy storms, will continue to shine brightly. Your light will pierce the darkness of the storms and bring a light of hope to others that are being overwhelmed by the storm's rising floodwaters.

Your faithful endurance will be a testimony for even the generations to follow. Your love will speak to even your children's children and beyond.

You are being built upon the solid rock. Trust me to excavate and to lay the proper foundation. A proper foundation will allow it's structure to stand.

Love, Dad

My Glory Will Be Revealed

"But the people's minds were hardened, and to this day whenever the old covenant is being read, the same veil covers their minds so they cannot understand the truth. And this veil can be removed only by believing in Christ." 2 Corinthians 3:14

My dear child,

Didn't I tell you that you would see my glory? Your belief has removed the veil that hardened hearts still wear. I paid the highest sacrificial price to tear that veil apart.

I am the same today, yesterday and forever. I am the Holy One. When I tore the veil of the temple, it wasn't a compromise of my holiness. My love for you paid the full price so the veil is no longer necessary.

The veil of separation has been replaced with the robe of relationship. My own son's blood covers you in *his* righteousness. Jesus' blood is your robe of adopted sonship!

His blood is your holiness. His sacrifice allows you to stand in my presence and see my glory. I faced intense disbelief and rejection from the religious who had lost sight of love.

Love is the unveiler! Love opens hearts! Love opens eyes! Love opens ears!

Love opened the tombs of the godly and shook the earth and restored life to godly men and women on the day that the veil was torn apart!

My glory was revealed. Sight was given to those who could not see. Hearing was given to those who lived in silence and separation was removed! Love gave you sonship. Love gave you relationship- a relationship that hears, sees and experiences my loving presence.

Let this love be evident to those around you who can only see the veil. Love broke through your veil. It will break through theirs as well.

The earth-shaking, rock-splitting, dead-raising Spirit of my love in your life may be unsettling for them. They are seeing my glory in you and my love will tear their veil.

Didn't I tell you that you would see my glory? My

glory unsettled you- it will unsettle them as well.

Love, Dad

Storms tell more than Stories

"He got up, rebuked the wind and said to the waves, "Quiet! Be still!" Then the wind died down and it was completely calm." Mark 4:33-34 NIV

Precious one,

I brought my disciples through a storm. Not just a typical rainstorm, but one that took them beyond their experience. I took them through a storm that brought them to the end of their fishermen's abilities. I took them into the storm in darkness. The intensity of the storm was such that all signs pointed to capsizing and the end of their lives. I brought them to the end of their faith- their faith in their own strength.

All the parables I told to the crowds, but my twelve men went through hands-on life training. Their experience as fishermen was insufficient and left them in fear.

Their self-reliance did not prepare them for my answer to their fearful cries. I didn't deliver them out of the storm. I changed their storm into peace. As I spoke, the storm was no more. My words of power and peace brought an immediate and intense calm.

The wind ceased! The seas went very calm! All of the panic, bailing, and shouting turned into silence.

My peace spoke louder than the storm. The storm didn't pass; it didn't move to another location. It ceased to be a storm. The storm had become peace.

Do not rely upon your ability to figure out your storm. Lean upon my ability to turn even the most life-shaking storm into peace that you could never explain.

Love, Dad

Another Storm?

"What do you mean, 'If I can'?" Jesus asked. "Anything is possible if a person believes." Mark 9:23

O child,

Does it seem that I have sent you out late in the evening on a boat headed into yet another storm? Does it feel as if I am lying asleep while you face the storm on your own? Is there a part of your heart that wonders if this storm could have been avoided if you had done something different earlier? Is there a part of you that wants to shout, "Thanks Father! I was really hoping for a safe and wonderful voyage because I'm with you! Now we're being pounded by another storm!"?

True faith will trust me; no matter how big or how frequent the storms. Am I worthy of your trust? A strong faith is one that has been exercised. A trained faith goes through the storms and holds on until I stand and shout "PEACE! BE STILL!"

Enduring faith will come out with wounds and battle scars. Every time I reach out my hand to you, I see the nail scars I carry and I am reminded how much I went through to show you my great love for you.

The wounds from your storms will heal, but let the

remaining scars remind you how I took you through the storm. Let them remind you how I brought peace and healing. Let those markings remind you of how your resemble your father.

Love, Dad

Stand and Believe

"But despite all the miraculous signs Jesus had done, most of the people still did not believe in him." John 12:37

My Child,

I have been digging deep into the soil of your life. Soil has to be broken through and soil has to be displaced in order for your foundation to be firmly and soundly connected to the solid rock.

I am the solid rock. I am not unstable ground that can be washed away by raging storms or rising floodwaters. I am the Rock. I am the rock that will give you the ability to stand.

Stand on my promises. They do not waiver and they do not change. The wind blows and will attempt to unsettle you. The rains will intensify and floodwaters will rise.

There will be storms of relentless intensity that cause even the firmest and most stubborn soil to become saturated until in finally gives way.

But I am the solid rock and the house that outlasts the storm shall be found to be firmly rooted and connected to me.

After disastrous storms, there are those who will

come and assess the damages and to find out what remains. Child, they won't recognize the terrain because the storm will have washed away the surface.

But what will be revealed is how your foundation has been firmly established upon the solid, permanent and unchangeable rock. What will be revealed is our relationship, our connection and my glory. When they walk up to the edge of the crevasse left from the passing storm, they will see that your foundation still stands firmly rooted upon me. Not only the foundation will remain, but also the structure built upon it will endure beyond the storm.

"When the floodwaters rise and break against that house, it stands firm because it *is* well built." (Luke 7:48)

Love, Dad

Blueprint of Love

"They said to each other, "Didn't our hearts burn within us as he talked with us on the road and explained the Scriptures to us?" Luke 24:32

Child,
When I created you, love was the reason. With my wisdom and understanding I designed you. My wisdom is the architect, the author, the loving designer whose heart leapt with uncontrollable joy as the blueprint of your life was so carefully drawn! Every detail is with great purpose and great intention. My love has been poured into every page of your blueprints.

There will be times when I will give you glimpses of

how the finished product will look. I will refresh your hope and encourage your faith.

I am the careful and wise engineer. In my love for you I have planned for the proper holes to be dug so that your life is built upon a sure foundation.

Do not be surprised by the structural requirements that call for excavation or removal of unstable soil. Don't lose sight of my love that tempers your soul's structural steel in heat and flames. I know what is required so that your life has strength to stand.

My love is always holding your blueprints- even when you don't understand. "Joyful are those who listen to me, watching daily at my gates, waiting outside my home!" (Psalm 8:34)

Child, trust my wisdom. Rely on my heart of love. Stay close to me. Seek my face every day. Remind yourself of my loving plans for you. Refresh your memory and let your heart be encouraged. Keep my promises ever in front of you so your joy will truly be your strength.

The digging, the excavating, the tempering and testing have incredible enduring value. My great love has orchestrated it all, so take heart. Be of great courage for I am building what I joyfully intended your life to be.

Love, Dad

Faith to Hold Course

Then Peter called to him, "Lord, if it's really you, tell me to come to you, walking on the water." Matthew 14:28

Faithful Child,

Hold Course! This is a leg of your journey where your sailing vessel must remain on proper course. Some may warn, "Do not sail past charted waters!" Yet they have not heard your "marching orders". Their concern is genuine and yes, there are perils to circumnavigate. But this does not mean to return to the safety of familiar landmarks and calm waters.

This is a season of great faith. This is a time for you to trust me and to hold the course I have prepared for you.

A pioneer will go into *new* places. A wise pioneer takes risks but relies heavily on what he knows and his past experiences that have carried him.

I am not sending you alone. I am your shepherd and I have gone before you. These may be completely uncharted waters and new territory for you, but I am the one who created the seas you sail upon.

This is a season when much of your familiar landmarks may be beyond your sight, but none-the-less, they are still there.

Great faith will require great risk and great trust in a great God. My promises remain to you as much as they were for my twelve men.

Great faith properly grounded in me shall carry you safely where I am taking you.

The pioneer's risk opens uncharted territory to those who will come behind him. Remember, a pioneer is no longer a pioneer if he settles. "Trust in the Lord with all your heart". (Proverbs 3:5) This is no time to lean upon your own wits, or your own feelings. Lean on me!

This is a season of great faith and great trust! Stay the

course!

Love, Dad

Learn From the Children Around You

"Children are a gift from the LORD; they are a reward from him." Psalm 127:3

My adopted one,
Learn all you can from the young children around you. Let their simple and loving trust be your example. Remember always that this is the faith that opens heaven's doors.

Young children will try your patience! They will wear you out! But remember how precious their hearts are to me! Always look for their trust and their confidence that comes from knowing to whom they belong!

They hold a precious example that speaks loudly to those who will listen. Child of mine, choose to listen to the voice that flows from a child's heart today.

Listen for my voice in theirs. Remember to whom you belong. Let their faith and trust be your example today.

You are greatly prized and loved and I always have my eye on you.

Love, Dad

Be Careful How You Hear

"So pay attention to how you hear. To those who listen to my teaching, more understanding will be given. But for those who are not listening, even what they think they understand will be taken away from them." Luke 8:18

My Child,
Not one moment of time you have spent with me is insignificant. Every moment I spend with you is very precious to me. You are the object of my affection- even when I am not the object of *your* affection.

My promise to you is love that never fails. I will love you in the midst of every moment and every event of your life. My love doesn't change- ever!

Adoption is always costly for the adopting parent. What great commitment of time, resources and love is required! How much love is needed to love a child that feels abandoned and unloved.

Your adoption cost my son's very life. No higher price could have been paid to adopt you, save you and bring you into my family.

Although your adoption cost me so much, it is my love gift for you. You could not repay me- not even in part!

But what great joy it gives me when you fully accept this gift- this priceless gift. How blessed I am when your sonship is evident- not in an arrogant pride, but in grateful humility.

When you choose to love me, my heart rejoices. When you choose to walk with me, I will reveal my heart to you.

Every moment we spend together is priceless,

precious and powerful. Don't ever think you have reached the highest place with me because there are always higher places we will go. There is always more I will reveal to you. Stay close and listen for my voice today.

Love, Dad

I Still Am

"Then Philip ran up to the chariot and heard the man reading Isaiah the prophet. "Do you understand what you are reading?" Philip asked, "How can I," he said, "unless someone explains it to me?" So he invited Philip to come up and sit with him. Then Philip began with that very passage of Scripture and told him the good news about Jesus.
As they traveled along the road, they came to some water and the eunuch said, "Look, here is water. What can stand in the way of my being baptized?"... Then both Philip and the eunuch went down into the water and Philip baptized him. When they came up out of the water, the Spirit of the Lord suddenly took Philip away, and the eunuch did not see him again, but went on his way rejoicing. Philip, however, appeared at Azotus and traveled about, preaching the gospel in all the towns until he reached Caesarea." Acts 8: 30-31, 36-40

Dear Child,
I am still the God of Isaiah and of Phillip as well! Words have poured forth to faithful men who desire to

hear my heart. Their desire was to know my desires for them and for the lives of those who need a touch of my presence and love.

Let my spirit come upon you. He is the One who moves in power. The very same power that holds the stars in their places can cause you to speak the good news and nothing can stand in the way of its power.

Walk with me and I will be able to take you to where the love, faith and hope I have given you to carry are needed-in the very moment it is needed.

Your obedient jar of clay carries my incredible power and life-changing presence.

Life-altering encounters await. You are the vessel that my spirit chooses to sail and to carry the precious cargo that will forever change the life-courses of many.

These are not casual, insignificant or coincidental connections. Carry this precious cargo with expectation and assurance for my Spirit's power will be released and it will satisfy longing hearts.

Remember the moon in the night sky is just an insignificant globe of dust, but when it is in the line of sight with the sun, it shines brilliantly into a darkened world. The moon has no brilliance of its own, yet when the sun pours its light upon it, it's reflective brilliance penetrates the darkness! It overcomes even the darkest of nights.

So walk in my sight today. Reflect the Son that shines upon your life. Walk in trust, in faith and in expectation. You will see what my glory will shine upon. You will shine and my glory will pierce the darkness. Walk with me today. Reflect my glory. Let my love overcome fear and darkness.

Love, Dad

Sent to Speak with Full Power

"For He is sent by God; He speaks God's words for God gives him the Spirit without limit." John 3:34

Dear one,
My words will not fail to accomplish what I spoke them to do. My words cannot fail to accomplish their purposes.

I am not a God of idle conversation but of purpose and power. Every spoken word, every preserved written word holds life, love and power.

Your unbelief will not negate any of my promises to you. Your failure to claim them will not change their value. You may miss out on their benefit, but they are still my promises and every promise I have spoken is yes and amen.

My promises are mine alone. Child, how I desire for you to hear my promises and to claim them every day! Joy comes to your journey when you know my promises and when you see them fulfilled.

Remember every word I speak holds promise and holds power. Walk closely with me today so you will hear my every word to you- promise, power and purpose!

Love, Dad

I Rejoice Over You

"At that same time Jesus was filled with the joy of the Holy Spirit, and he said, "O Father, Lord of heaven and earth, thank you for hiding these things from those who think themselves wise and clever, and for revealing them to the childlike. Yes, Father, it pleased you to do it this way." Luke 10:21

Child,
Remember how I rejoice over you. What joy is mine when your heart responds to the treasures of heaven! When your heart is responsive to mine, you will receive these treasures. This world is full of distractions, yet those who truly seek me will truly find me.

I will open my heart to you and share deep things with you. This is my love gift to you. People will see my character traits in you. They will see wisdom, truth, and patience. They will see these things because of our relationship. Your life will be salt upon theirs; creating thirst for what you carry.

Remember my love for you never changes- even when your circumstances and situations may attempt to tell you the contrary.

Don't allow difficulty or hardship to cause you to feel as if you have wandered. Don't allow life's pressures to make you think they are the result of your sinful error. Yes, some hardships are the result of your selfish, sinful choices. But there are some that are not!

Some of these difficulties are simply preparation for the journey ahead. Others are the enemy's attempts to instill fear and doubt within you.

Remember my promise to be with you! Remember my promise to cause all things to work toward good in your life.

> Life's trials cannot change my promises!
> Satan himself cannot change my promises!
> Your doubt and fear cannot change my promises!

Let my river cut its course; let it wash away what I

desire to remove. It flows in great love and with great purpose.

Fear not the storm! The greater the storm, the greater changes will be accomplished. The greatest storms shall gain the attention of many.

I never cease to rejoice over you!

Love, Dad

My Fullness Fully Dwells

"Bring all the tithes into the storehouse so there will be enough food in my Temple. If you do," says the LORD of Heaven's Armies, "I will open the windows of heaven for you. I will pour out a blessing so great you won't have enough room to take it in! Try it! Put me to the test!" Malachi 3:10

Oh my unsure one,

Yes, the windows of heaven are ready to open over you! Your clay jar will always be just a clay jar. As long as you are on this side of heaven, your clay jar will always be a clay jar.

Yet you have been chosen to carry my glory. My spirit shines within you with full brilliance! Does it surprise you when others see my glory within you? I want you to share in this glory with me as you faithfully carry what I have placed within you.

My full-ness- all that I am is my Spirit. I have fully entered you and fully reside within you. Fully, completely and holding nothing back! I am limited only by your doubt to step out and trust me. There will be times that I will prompt your heart to pray over others and you will see my power. Listen closely for my voice. It is the voice of the Solid Rock. You will know my voice and as you pray over them my Spirit will heal hearts, souls and bodies. Tears will flow from their brokenness, but my Spirit will move with your words and actions to be the balm that brings healing, soothing and comfort.

Your faith-filled obedient spirit that has joined with my Spirit will restore lives.

This is nothing short of a miracle. It is the miracle that will open your heart to many more. So remind yourself often that our spirits are united and this relationship is forever.

So when I prompt your heart, do not shrink back. Rather, step out, take the risk and I will always meet your faith with my loving power.

I dwell in your for great purposes; very great! One of the greatest is that of relationship. You no longer are a slave, but a dear son! This Father desires for you to experience the depths of this relationship every day. Do not shrink back, but instead jump out in extravagant joy-filled faith!

Love, Dad

Stand Firm, Soldier

"Therefore put on the full armor of God, so that when the day of evil comes, you may be able to stand your ground, and after you have done everything, to stand." Ephesians 6:13 NIV

"And so, dear brothers and sisters, I plead with you to give your bodies to God because of all he has done for you. Let them be a living and holy sacrifice--the kind he will find acceptable. This is truly the way to worship him." Romans 12:1

Child,
You are called to be my holy and acceptable sacrifice.

A soldier that hides from the battle may preserve his life, but in his fear and desire for peaceful safety has cancelled his sacrifice to his commanding officer. Where is his acceptable sacrifice? How can he celebrate victory over the enemy if he did not stand?

I do not send my soldiers into battle without full provision. Be strong in me and in my mighty power. Put on my armor- not your own armor, put on mine!

My armor is perfect and complete and will do all that I purpose for it to do. Stand your ground! You stand on holy ground when you stand firm where I call you to stand.

I have given you my full armor. When the enemy looks in your direction, fear grips his heart because he sees my glorious armor!

You are fully clad in the truth of my promises! As you claim them you become clad in my armor.

My armor never fails. So do not fail to stand the ground on which I have called you to stand. Hold high your shield of faith. Affirm your confidence in the one who sent you! Hold your shield of faith high!

The enemy not only shoots arrows but also has set them aflame in attempt to burn away the safety of your surroundings. But trust your commander's faithful promises and stand firm!

How I desire for you to experience victory with me!

These battles carry such intensity and will leave you wounded, yet do not fear. I hold out my nail-scarred hands to you and give you my promise to always be with you.

Stand firm! Hold your ground! Victory comes to those that are still standing after the battle has ceased. Be a living and holy sacrificial soldier for me!

Love, Dad

Am I Your First Love?

"Yet I hold this against you: You have forsaken the love you had at first...". Revelation 2:4 NIV

Child,

You can know all about me, obey all the religious rules and attempt to keep your self acceptable in my sight. You can strive to study and get it all exactly right so that your theology is clear and straight, yet I am after your heart.

Where you heart is, your treasure resides. If your heart is after correct theology, then correct theology may be your treasure.

My treasure is you! Am I your treasure? Am I your first love?

Go back to what you heard and believed at first. Hold to it firmly. Relationship without love turns into religious responsibility. When your heart has lost sight of love, fear will creep in and cause you to doubt. Fear will cause you to try to fix the lack of love by seeking my approval by religion.

Child, remember your first love. Remember my Spirit

that dwells within you! Don't let all the religious activities crowd out our father-child relationship. All of your busyness will not change my love for you.

Keep our love first and foremost in your life. Instead of striving to get it all correct, look for my love as you study my word! Return to the joy of your first love!

You are so greatly loved,
Love, Dad

My Words Are Forever

"Heaven and earth will pass away, but my words will never pass away." Luke 21:33 NIV

My Child,
Faithless men put trust in only what they can touch, handle or feel. They base their existence and their purpose upon the temporary- the non-eternal. My words- every one of them is forever. Every promise and every truth is worthy of your faith and your trust.

The words I spoke to Abraham still *are*. Those I spoke to Moses, Joshua, Samuel and David still *are*.

I am the God who *is*! Every word that comes from my mouth is wise and it is worthy of your hearing.

I am still the God who speaks. Those that seek to that the heart of the Lord will not be disappointed. I will open the deep things of my heart to those whose hearts are fully mine.

I spoke the heavens and earth into existence. I spoke all life into being. I breathed my own breath in man. I ordained the day for you to come into existence! I am the one who opened your eyes to see, your ears to hear and your heart to respond to my great love for you.

Keep your eyes on me; keep your ears attentive to my voice. Keep your heart unattached from this world's distractions and detours. Do not let them pull your faith away to be placed onto that which is only temporary.

Remember when my Son shouted, "It is finished!" I tore the curtain in the temple. I completely destroyed the separation between you and me! I, your eternal, wise, creator-dad and loving Father have removed the barrier between eternity and the temporary. Let me speak words from eternity into your temporal life. My words are life. They are eternal life! I am the One who opened your eyes and ears so you can share in my joy, my love and my glory!

What a good day to hear, to see and to respond! The promises you carry also carry this life. You carry this treasure so get ready for when I prompt you.

I will show you where, when and how to impart this upon others. Be ready!

Love, Dad

Turn Back to Your First Love

"We love each other because he loved us first."
1 John 4:19 NIV

Dear Child,

I have pursued you with my love. Child, not only were you conceived in love, but love was the driving force in my heart when I first spoke your name.

Long before you came into existence, my heart was full of love and joy as my thoughts and plans for you were first spoken and written in my book.

As my thoughts of love for your were written, I knew every detail about you. How I was overwhelmed with joy as I designed your heart to respond to me in a way that is uniquely and deeply personal and intimate!

I have never departed from my first love for you. What joy you give me when your heart remembers and resounds your first love for me! Your first love for me was genuine, humble and honest. You had nothing to give to me. You came and took my hand and let me wash you completely clean of your sinful past.

O child, always remember and rejoice in our first love. Keep songs of praise flowing from your heart. Keep my promises on your lips. These are the works you did at first. Your heart could not help but do them!

Keep my praises flowing and remember my promises and they will drown out the deceitful and alluring melody of the temptresses that are jealous of our love for each other.

Do not fear to walk in the spiritual realm with me. Walk with me in close, loving and intimate communion. My Spirit has become one with yours! Let the joyous song of praise overcome any attempt to pull us apart.

The song of our first love cannot be imitated. Keep it in your heart and upon your tongue. I truly dwell in your praises! Child I have never lost my first love for you!

Love, Dad

Buried Truth

"Then he added, "Every teacher of religious law who

becomes a disciple in the Kingdom of Heaven is like a homeowner who brings from his storeroom new gems of truth as well as old." Matthew 13:52

My Precious Child,
I am the revealer of truth. I am the One who is truth.

I planted seeds of truth in the prepared, fertile soil of your heart. A farmer plants different kinds of seeds and they will all grow differently. Some will sprout quickly while others will stay hidden deep in the soil for an extended period of time.

But the wise farmer will plant those important seeds much earlier than when he desires their harvest. He knows those special seeds need much more time in the ground, but he plants early and is willing to patiently wait for them to sprout, to grow and to bloom.

There are seeds of my truth that have been planted deep within the soil of your heart. When I placed them there, you received them with a joyful and receptive heart. You rejoiced knowing I had entrusted and revealed them to you. Yet there is explosive growth to come!

As you remain faithful to me, as you stay close beside my river of living water, those seeds of truth that were planted deep in your soul long ago will burst open with new life! It has been my intention all along that they sprout, grow tall and produce much fruit.

So do not lose heart in the waiting. Hold tight to my promises. Stay close to the living water of my Spirit and do not lose heart- even when the wait is long and when other crops have grown up quickly and already have been harvested.

Hold fast to my promise to you. I, your father, am a wise farmer and I have planted those important seeds exactly where and when I wanted them to be planted.

So do not lose heart and do not forget my promises are true. The seeds of truth I have buried deep within you will burst forth with new life and valuable fruit. Your perseverance and faithfulness will be celebrated both in heaven and on earth.

Your steadfast, faithful trust in my timing and my wisdom will be a shining light of hope and a power-filled testimony to those that grow weary in the waiting.

Do not lose heart! Keep your eyes on me! It is very much worth the wait, so wait with expectation!

Love, Dad

Pressed On Every Side

"We are pressed on every side by troubles, but we are not crushed. " 2 Corinthians 4:8

Child of mine,
Did I not tell you in the world you would find trouble? This world- my own creation- gave me trouble and opposition to the point of death.

I was pressed from every side. I was surrounded in the walls of death, yet I was not crushed. My faithful obedience to my father sent me to be pressed by your sins. Child, the penalties for your sins I willingly took upon myself to pay your fines and penalties that my righteousness demands. In my deep love for you, I bore the burden and the weight of the penalty of death that was meant for you.

The greatest weight of your sins pressed me from every side. The enemy sought to destroy me. But the enemy's attempt to destroy I used for my victory!

Just as intense pressures and heat will cause diamond to form from carbon, so was my glorious victory over the pressure and heat of your sin. The enemy's attempt to crush me became my victory. Victory that shines with unparalleled beauty! Victory that is priceless! My victory paid your penalty and set you free.

So when you, child, are pressed from every side, when you are unfairly and unjustly pressed- remember my promise that you will not be crushed. Remember my victory. Remember how brilliant diamonds are forged under great pressure!

I could simply tell you about my victory, but how much deeper is your understanding and heart connection when I allow you to experience the victory that comes when you faithfully endure being pressed from every side.

Child, this too, is a part of my love. Even though it is unpleasant and pain-filled, it is still a very important part of my love. This is the part that wants to share some of the deepest parts of my heart with you.

Diamonds are formed from intense heat and pressure. They not only hold incomparable value, but they are unbreakable and unalterable!

Do not lose heart, my child. Just stay close to mine.

Love, Dad

Light That Overcomes

"The light shines in the darkness, and the darkness can never extinguish it." John 1:5

My busy Child,

Think about a sunrise. Every day my light overcomes the darkness of night. Darkness must always give way to the light of day. The darkness of night only returns after the light has moved on. Darkness can never overcome the light- ever!

This is a truth I put in place from the beginning of my creation of all the heavens and the earth. The darkest of nights cannot overcome the light.

Sunrise is my promise to you. Even the longest of nights cannot stop the rising of the sun.

Men love the darkness more than the light. They will run to the shadows to hide and find others hiding there as well.

Let each morning sunrise remind you of my faithfulness to you. Let each sunrise remind you how far into the darkness my love can reach.

This is so easily missed because it can become routine and ordinary. The sun will rise just as it has everyday of your life. But that is no reason to overlook it or forget the promise and blessing it brings.

Let each sunrise remind you of my promises to you. Do not let my promises become commonplace. Great is my love for you! Great are my promises to you! Remind your heart and rejoice!

Love, Dad

Stay Close and Listen

"What I tell you now in the darkness, shout abroad

when daybreak comes. What I whisper in your ear, shout from the housetops for all to hear!" Matthew 10:27

Child,

Stay close to me so that you always hear what I whisper to you. The cries and shouts of the world will try to overpower you and attempt to pull you away. But stay close to me and you will always be able to hear my call.

Do not believe the Liar who attempts to make you believe that I have left you to fend for yourself. I am with you always! There is never a time when I am not with you. My love for you never fails to love you.

The enemy points out your sin and failures. How he wants you to be overcome by your sinfulness. He knows and will accuse you and tell you that you are unworthy and unacceptable to enter my presence.

Don't listen to his accusations! The price has been fully paid. I have fully paid the debt and penalty for your sin.

All he can do now is shout and accuse that you're not worthy to my love-gift. The truth is you're not worthy! On your own, you never would be worthy!

But this is my gift of love to you. Remember, a gift is never earned. What is earned is called a wage. Your wages for your sin is the same as for every other's. Your wages for your sin would be death. But my gift is given from a father's heart that is *full* of compassion. My gift is eternal relationship with me.

My gift washes you in my perfect love. Stay close to me. The enemy fears me, so stay close!

There is power in my presence, so stay close to me. There is purpose in my presence so stay close so you will know it. There is peace in my presence because fear has to flee. There is protection in my presence for you are my dear adopted child! Stay close to me today.

Love, Dad

You are Well-Built and Well-Planned

"And I am certain that God, who began the good work within you, will continue his work until it is finally finished on the day when Christ Jesus returns." Philippians 1:6

Dear one,
How I desire to be the cornerstone that you build your life upon. There are many that attempt to build their lives without the true cornerstone.

Child, I have laid the plans that carry your name. I wrote detailed plans for your existence with great purpose, great forethought, and great love. I wrote them with great intention in my book.

Do not let your disbelief hold you captive any longer. Why do you doubt that the "LORD of Heaven's armies" has such a great personal interest and deep love for you?

Don't let feelings of unworthiness or unimportance keep your heart imprisoned another moment! Let your faith arise above the doubts!

Yes, I wrote plans that carry your name. They are set apart from all others. They are the ones I wrote expressly for you.

I am the rock upon which you will be built. I am the builder, the master craftsman that will build it, as well. Even more, I am your cornerstone that is placed perfectly. It is aligned, leveled and firmly set.

With me as your cornerstone, your walls will have the proper reference that will allow them to be placed in such a way that they will stand strong.

The cornerstone is always there and never changes. It will be the *true* reference point for every other stone that is placed in the structure of your life.

The cornerstone will remove the doubts. You will *know,* you will find peace and you always have assurance that I am placing each stone in its proper location.

The cornerstone is your anchor in the storm. It is your anchor that others, who are in their storm of discouragement or trial, need to see.

Your faith-filled trust in me will renew hope and trust in those who are in the midst of overwhelming storms.

Child, I have placed great purpose within you. Never doubt your importance to me.

Love, Dad

Many Trials for a Little While

"So be truly glad. There is wonderful joy ahead, even though you have to endure many trials for a little while." 1 Peter 1:6

My weary child,

Does it seem as if all of hell has opened over you? Does is feel as if your trials are delivered in large bunches? Does it seem like this storm is too great for you to handle? Why do your doubt my continual presence with you?

I will use *all* things. I will use every last thing in your life to create good in you. " All things" means exactly that- *all* things!

Remember, the more intense the storm, the greater your faith's strength can be.

I have called you to captain your "faith-vessel" and as you stand through these storms, those around you will see that your faith is not in vain. You show them how your trust will allow my good to come even in the most intense of storms. Your example of standing in faith is an inheritance for those who look up to you and for those who come this way after you.

My Captain, stand in this storm!

Love, Dad

Gold Worth Mining

Reverence for the LORD is pure,
lasting forever. The laws of the LORD are true;
each one is fair. They are more desirable than gold,
even the finest gold. They are sweeter than honey, even
honey dripping from the comb.

Psalm 19: 10-11

Child,

My word stands forever and I still breathe life into hearts that are fully mine. My every breath and every word hold deep purpose.

Consider one who searches for gold. He pays attention to the identifying signs that show gold is nearby. The wise miner will not ignore those signs, but will stay there and dig deeper and his diligence will reap great dividends.

But consider the casual hiker that may miss those very important signs. He may walk directly over and miss completely the treasure that could be his!

Listen closely to when my spirit speaks to your heart so you will not miss those treasures that have been carefully placed along the path of your journey.

There will be effort and perseverance required at times to unearth these blessings, but my word stands forever. Abundant blessings are marked and set aside for you.

"Angels are eagerly watching!" (1Peter 1:12)
So am I!

Love, Dad

Listen for Me

"So we must listen very carefully to the truth we have heard, or we may drift away from it." Hebrews 2:1

My child,

Yes, do listen for my voice today! The deceiver has planted a lie in many hearts. He has planted the lie that I am far off from you and have turned my back toward you.

These seeds can take root and feed upon men's sinfulness. His choking weeds can overcome the seeds of truth that I have planted in your heart.

It is imperative that you, my dear child, listen for my voice every day.

Oh, the joys of those who do not follow wicked

advice, but whose delight is in listening for my voice.

That is where my river flows with the water of the Holy Spirit. The water of my Spirit can break the nutrients out of even the dead leaves that have fallen from your branches.

A tree that remains planted by my river is the tree whose roots go down deep. Much deeper than the roots of the enemy's weeds!

Listen for my voice every day. Let your roots go down deep and I will refresh you every day.

When your roots have been established in deep soil, you will bear the fruit I intended for you to produce!

This is such a basic and obvious fact yet so many miss it because they fear the fast-growing weeds that flower and prosper quicker than they. Some let impatience uproot them to wander away and seek something or somewhere else than the river of my Spirit.

The tree that remains planted by my Spirit's river of living water will be ever-green and will bear its fruit in every season. So do not let impatience cause you to envy the fast-growing weeds of the wicked around you. Their growth will soon fade and the wind will simply blow them away from your presence.

Listen for my voice today! Listen for the rush of water I send to refresh and revive you every day. I am the one that causes your roots to grow deep and strong. Consider a giant Sequoia tree. It patiently grows over years, over decades- even over centuries. See how it has become established and well-rooted.

Stay patient, stay faithful and listen for my voice today. Do not harden your heart, but instead receive. Your faithfulness will see growth like the Sequoia. Faith that the years, decades and centuries cannot help but notice! They will respond in awe and give me the glory.

So listen for my voice today. My every word is life-packed!

Love, Dad

Adopted to Full Inheritance

"Now you are no longer a slave but God's own child. And since you are his child, God has made you his heir." Galatians 4:7

My adopted child,

A good father gives his children good gifts. I, your Heavenly Father give you gifts that are much more than good. They are heavenly.

You have been adopted fully. Not in only a part, not just in contract, but adopted in full- in my full love.

I paid the highest price to adopt you. Think about what a mere man has to expend to adopt a child. Think about how much time, expense and dedication of his heart goes into adopting the child he has grown to love.

Think about how he has to prove to the governing authorities that he is worthy to be trusted to be a proper guardian and parent.

His love for that child is truly tested and challenged to see if his love is deep enough. Those authorities know that if it is costly, his love will be truly proven.

I paid the highest price to set you free from the orphaned life you once lived. My love was proven by how much your adoption cost me!

The greatest gift I give you is Holy Spirit who dwells in your very heart. I placed him in your heart with very great intention. I could have placed my Spirit in your mind so you could comprehend the knowledge of your sonship.

But I have placed my Spirit within your heart because even thought it cost me everything, I want you to know my great love for you. I would do it all over again for you, child!

You are now my child. This is why I rejoice! Now never do we have to live apart from one another. Now we can spend our days in ever-deepening father-child relationship!

You are my child and I won't hold back all that I have for you. You are fully adopted, fully paid for, fully loved, and fully my heir!

I am much more than a good father. Much, much more! All the depths of the riches of Heaven are your inheritance.

Know too, that some of the most prized treasures of Heaven may come through struggle or pain. Yet my love for your never waivers. I love you enough to expose you to trials so your understanding of how strong my love for you truly is!

My love for you has no limit. I didn't give up on the pain-filled journey to the cross. I was going to rescue you and adopt you no matter what the cost!

My heart for you is to understand love that does not give up. I want you to grasp love that never quits, which will pay *any* cost. This is the most precious gift a father can give- his heart and his love. No matter what!

You are greatly loved and greatly prized, my adopted one!

Love, Dad

Free to Choose

"It was for freedom that Christ set us free; therefore keep standing firm and do not be subject again to a yoke of slavery." Galatians 5:1NIV

My child,

You are no longer a slave, but a free man. The full price for your freedom had been paid- completely!

A free man is free to choose for himself. Just as the prodigal son was free to choose, so are you. The prodigal was free before he left his father's presence, yet he failed to recognize his freedom. He saw the walls of his father's house as restraints. He felt as if they were walls of a prison. The fences at the property lines were, to him, keeping him from being truly free.

But his wise father had built strong walls to protect his son. He put up fences not to restrain his son, but to let all evil doers on the outside know that if they brought their wicked ways inside that boundary, they would have to deal with a very protective father!

Yet the son was free to choose whether to stay or to leave because he was not a slave but a son. You are a son as well!

In the presence of the father were protection, provision, purpose, promise and peace. Where the father was not present the son found only self-destruction and dissatisfaction. He found hunger for home!

You are free to choose, child. How I desire for you to stay with me today!

There will always be times that require hard work and perseverance. Let's face them together! Let's celebrate the joy-filled satisfaction that comes on the other side of endurance.

I will not demand for you to stay. I will not demand for you to go through these struggles with me. But child remember how much closer you are to someone after you have endured a struggle *together*. My desire is that not that you just make it through, but that our relationship deepens as a result.

You are free to choose. My heart is that you remain here and face what this day brings together with me.

Love, Dad

No Strings Attached

"You once walked, following the course of this world, following the prince of the power of the air, the spirit that is now at work in the sons of disobedience."
Ephesians 2:2 ESV

Dear one,

I am the one true God. There is no other in existence. The deceiver attempts to make himself appear as a powerful god, but he is merely a disowned and disgruntled prince who has been disinherited from me. His only rewards are pain, suffering, misery and death. He is *not* a god but only a prince.

You, child, do not have to answer to him or any other so-called, non-existing god that he puts in front of you. Don't give it any credence because it is only a puppet or marionette with strings controlled by the deceiver.

He may be a talented puppeteer, but he is not a god. And make no mistake: he is a fallen prince and there are spirits with evil intent.

I, your father, am the one true God. I have set you free with no strings attached. The enemy tries to make you believe his lie that says there are strings attached- that my strings are more like ropes that will bind you. But there are no strings attached!

No strings, but I long to embrace you in my arms of love. I don't want you to be my puppet that is controlled by my every whim. I long to see you accept my loving embrace and remain in my presence.

Nothing frustrates the enemy more than when he sees my children resembling their father! How he envies my adopted ones reacting to my loving embraces!

No, you are not a puppet. You are a child set free to run and to dance with joy in my presence. A puppet cannot think for itself- it hasn't life. But you are my child!

How great is this father's love for you! Run and dance in your sonship today! I dance over you with joy!

Love, Dad

Faith Refined

"Take the impurities out of silver, and a vessel is ready for the silversmith to mold." Proverbs 25:4 GWT

Dear one,
I am refining your faith in me. Not your personality; I am refining your *faith* in me.

As the intensity of my refining fire rises, it will cause impurities within to rise to the surface. My refiner's fire may come through trials and times of long perseverance.

But know that in my great love for you I will use the intense heat to remove all that is not faith.

The refiner's fire will burn away self-confidence and pride. Such intense heat is required to loosen the impurities until all that remains is pure- pure faith. This is faith that shines and is gloriously brilliant. It is so brilliant that it reflects perfectly the image of the refiner!

My refiner's fire will bring the impurities up to the surface. When it does, do not lose your hope in my promise. Do not focus on what has come to the surface, but choose to focus on my promise. Focus on my refiner's promise. I am refining your faith in me. Far below the surface refining will start even before it becomes evident on the surface.

Pure genuine faith in me, especially in times of faith-refinement, is so very critical. Know, too, that even though at times you feel without faith, you *do* have it! I see it in you! I do not refine gold if there isn't any gold to refine! I see the precious faith-gold within you and I know its incredible value. It is worth the trials and the pain that will cause your faith to stand alone, to shine, and to reflect my glory!

Trust me in this: As you allow me to refine your faith as gold is refined in fire, I am a careful, attentive and loving faith-goldsmith. I am beginning to see my reflection in your faith-gold and it brings me such joy!

Love, Dad

Turn Your Heart Toward Me

"Then Peter called to him, "Lord, if it's really you,

tell me to come to you, walking on the water." "Yes, come," Jesus said.

So Peter went over the side of the boat and walked on the water toward Jesus. But when he saw the strong wind and the waves, he was terrified and began to sink. "Save me, Lord!" he shouted." Matthew 14:28-30

My Child,

You could get up and face the day without me. You could get going on your long to-do list and face all your obligations, expectations and plans on your own.

This is the moment where idolatry starts. This is where you lose sight of my great love for you. This is the moment where Peter began to sink into the water and away from his faith in me. This is the moment where his water-walk turned into fear of drowning.

The moment your actions tell me, "Father, I have so much to do today and deadlines are screaming for my obedience. If I don't buckle down and take control of it all, it won't get done. I am too busy to sit at your feet, Father!" Do you realize your heart is allowing the cares of this world to take top priority?

Child, this is where idolatry takes root. Do you really want your worries to take the throne and to take control today?

Child, reaffirm your confidence and trust in me today. I am the One who designed and planned your life in deep love and intricate care. Spend time with me in these early moments. Let me remind you of my great love for you. Let me show you how my mercies to you are truly new every day. Let me wash your heart and your mind with my presence like the sunrise washes over the mountains and fills the earth with its warmth and light. Let my light chase away the fear and doubt of darkness.

This day holds no surprises for me. It holds no panic for me. The eager, self-reliant sheep that runs off ahead his shepherd will miss out on the peace and protection that comes from walking closely with the shepherd.

My heart's desire is that you turn you gaze to me. My heart for you is that your strength for the day is found in my presence and your day be spent with me. Wherever we go, let's go together.

Reaffirm your trust in me today and you will find me worthy of your trust.

That night that I called Peter to come and walk with me on the water, he did so until he focused on the wind and waves and took his eyes off me. But even still when he began to become overwhelmed by the situation, he still turned toward me. He could have turned away and swam for his life to reach the boat again. Yet Peter knew where he needed to turn. Even in his failure Peter knew to turn to me.

Walk with me today, child. Enjoy my peace, my protection and my presence.

Love, Dad

Mark Well the Path on Which You Came

"Set up road signs; put up guideposts. Mark well the path by which you came." Jeremiah 31:21

Child,

Your journey is to be signposts for those who will come after you. What blessing is lost if you walk this journey with me but neglect to "mark well the path by which you came".

Think about the times on this journey when you cried to me for a signpost. Think about the times when the journey was long and you needed reassurance. Remember those times when you were uncertain and weary and you cried for a signpost that would keep your hope alive.

There are ones who will be upon this same path and child my desire is that you mark this path well.

These signposts are their inheritance so mark well the path from which you came.

Love, Dad.

WHY I JOURNAL THE JOURNEY

My journals have become a vital part of my alone-times with Jesus. My journals have become important to me just like a good, strong canvas bag is important for a gold miner to carry his priceless nuggets.

The miner's bag needs to be strong, long-lasting and readily available. I have found that if I don't write these precious letters from Dad down, they'd soon be forgotten. I don't ever want to forget even the smallest of gems he has uncovered!

I believe that God has put a deep desire within my soul to write, to record, and to draw. It's been placed there to leave a legacy of the revelation of God's heart that is filled with such a great love for his adopted children.

This great love never ceases, never fails and never diminishes. His love shines through when this life's journey is easy and it shines through just as brilliantly when life is overwhelmingly difficult.

My journaling is the result of my taking God up on his promise- if I draw near to him, he will draw near to me. "Come close to God and He will come close to you". James 4:8

He has become incredibly true to his word. "He confides in those who fear him." Psalm 25:10

My journals, too, will reveal how he allowed me to pour out my heart to him over and over again. But more importantly, they show when God taught me to wait upon him. He began to speak to my heart and I began to write what my heart heard.

I am taking my father up on his truth: "My sheep know my voice and I know theirs." (John 10:27) So I continue to journal this journey of an ever-deepening love relationship with Dad.

I pray that my journey with him would ignite the same desire to follow hard after Jesus within you, dear reader.

Seek him as fine gold! Don't give up if it gets difficult, gold mining takes diligence and perseverance! Press on, keep seeking him!

He is truly a "rewarder of those who diligently seek him." (Hebrews 11:6)

Remember, you may just have a shovel and a gold pan and diligence will be rewarded!

Go for the gold that is waiting for you in relationship with a very loving, very personal, and very amazing heavenly father.

Journaling the journey,

Ken

www.ingramcontent.com/pod-product-compliance
Lightning Source LLC
Chambersburg PA
CBHW061454040426
42450CB00007B/1352